C000006626

WE ARE NOW APPROACHING

WILL STEVENSON

Bent Key Publishing

First published in Great Britain by Bent Key Publishing, 2023
Copyright © Will Stevenson, 2023
The moral right of the author has been asserted.

All rights reserved. No part of this book may be reproduced in any form or by any electronic or mechanical means, including information storage and retrieval systems, without permission in writing from the publisher, except by reviewers, who may quote brief passages in a review.

ISBN: 978-1-915320-21-6

Bent Key Publishing
Office 2, Unit 5 Palatine Industrial Estate
Causeway Avenue
Warrington WA4 6QQ
bentkeypublishing.co.uk

Edited by Rebecca Kenny @ Bent Key
Cover art © Samantha Sanderson-Marshall @ SMASH Design and Illustration
smashdesigns.co.uk

Printed in the UK by Mixam UK Ltd.

This is a book for transient people

CONTENTS

Preface   *vii*

i. We Are Now Approaching   11

ii. Leaving the Station   55

Acknowledgements / About the Author   97
About Bent Key   100

PREFACE

On the train, eyes closed: Victorian oak, feather quills, Brontë. Blink: rattling metal sheets and bedraggled, crescent faced commuters. *The Metro*, glum coffee cups, chewing gum. I stand up to write. I stand up on packed-out sunrise buses moving down train tracks because there aren't enough services; in smoking shelters; outside McDonald's. In each of these places, I worry that I have nothing to say. That the promise I have made is an empty one. I think about the order in which these poems will come into your life. I don't think it will reflect the order in which they came into mine. I don't think all art needs to have a through line, a neon sign that blinks down above tin-pan streets, back alleys, directing you to emote with me. I'd probably write about 'ginnels' now, but I wouldn't say it out loud. I've lived in Manchester since 2015. With strangers who became dreams who became ghosts. With friends who became strangers at three in the morning. In high-rise flats and rag n' bone estates, in the centre of a city coated in bruised silver armour. Three careers, two universities. Midnight shifts skipping bin bags over my head, hoping they don't split. Lived in what an American would call a suburb, a satellite state caught between a cultural powerhouse and a fading legacy.

In 2014, I took my first train from Skegness to Manchester with my Dad. I tasted the Northern graffiti off Oxford Road and I leant into it, sticking my nose to the creative scaffolding of the city. We took the train a lot when we were kids: Dad was a signalman, a job that won't exist for much longer. I wonder when the longing stops: we're already nostalgic for Blairism, bobs and tank tops. I think a lot about this and I am scared of culture running out. It seems to me that we've recycled our ideas because we don't have many left; ever since Elvis we've been on a spin cycle. It's not like there was much culture to be borrowed in the 50s. The turn of the century in 1900 seemed to mark a cultural reset: deposed monarchs, new music, a shaking-off of an oppressive establishment culture that we are now leaning ever closer towards. Two separate worlds are forming and most people skate on the dividing line between them, pulled in one direction or another by their algorithms. The programmer carries a heavy burden.

Manchester let me in and let me breathe. Before then, I'm not certain I had lived at all.

WE ARE NOW APPROACHING

I.
WE ARE NOW
APPROACHING

All the stops along the way

ROBOT WARS AND YOUR LIQUORICE (PRELUDE)

In the nineties, we lived next to a fruit shop
That was really a florist
A child has no need for flowers
So I christened it The Fruit Market

I should have bought out the boutique,
Swapped shiny pennies for the bricks
Plucked you every flower
Filled up the bath with a watering can

Sheared the moss sloping up
Our red brick walls and circumstance:
Headaches, hazy hospital whites, basements
Breached with flash-flood emotion distracted us

One summer, at a social club
That's since been turned to dust,
I pulled plasticine people
Into my silent TV dinners

Flicked endless yellow stars onto
Shiny black rock, moulded
Loneliness into permanent
Thick paint.

These memories taste like sweet and sour
Chips and batter bits – deep fried and thick
Strained in that shabby colander, served on
ASDA white-porcelain

In the window, a younger me watches
BBC Two on a sofa in the dark:
Six o' clock carnage, yellow-bellied cartoons,
Liquorice then lights out

I remember when Bassetts
Sent us the new Sports Mix
I thought we were sweet-shop royalty:
The most important family in the country

Someone Important knew about our tradition!
Robot Wars and liquorice — our tiny isolation,
When no new textures worked for me
I knew they'd halt production

Three months later, the Sports Mix hit the shops
They stopped airing Robot Wars
I grew out of liquorice
I never plucked the flowers

A DECADE COMPRESSED

The next train arriving on Platform One will be:

Skegness > Nottingham
Skegness > Nottingham > Manchester Oxford Road
Skegness > Nottingham > Salford Crescent
Skegness > Nottingham > Manchester Piccadilly
Manchester Piccadilly > Liverpool Lime Street > Ormskirk
Ormskirk > Liverpool Lime Street > Manchester Piccadilly
Manchester Piccadilly > London King's Cross
Manchester Piccadilly > Glasgow > Aberdeen
Aberdeen > Glasgow > Manchester Oxford Road
Manchester Piccadilly > Glossop
Manchester Oxford Road > Bolton
Bolton > Levenshulme
Present > Future

CHRISTMAS IN JULY

for my brother, Ben

We turned out the back of the big airing cupboard.
I saw the sweat dripping from your odd-one-out hair
Whilst we tussled with the Christmas Tree
One Tuesday in July, the lights inside the boxes
Nearly decapitated us as we celebrated
The End Of All Wars, and prayed inside for our Yuletide blessings
To start early this year
We took the batteries from our remote and put them
Into the Snowman — it still didn't dance and no-one celebrated
Our Christmas like we did
Wrapped in half-smashed light bulb strips

SIX THOUSAND DAYS

Six thousand days
with these bones
pressed into leather
The county lines of farm country stretch
across satellite screens
I play eye spy
in cityscapes I dream of
touching
I have made it to three
cultural fault lines
yet to seep into my home,
connected with the grass
by oxygen and nothing more
I am swallowed inside of silos
and I am waiting for
the free fall
My future is tea-
stained and I do not know
how many mugs I will yet knock over
Searching for all-night diners

SOMETIMES

i've been sinking ships in my living room
drainpipe jeans and whiskey bottles
holes in second-hand sofa seams
adjust unpaid subscriptions thrust
under door stops
some times my glottal stops and
sometimes it does not
i cannot trace my childhood
the paper is drawn too thick and
all the lead in the pencil keeps snapping
when i draw over it comes undone
looking more like a squiggle instead of a sun
i've been sinking ships in my living room

ON HOLIDAY IN THE MIDLANDS

In the summer of 2016, I worked in a holiday camp
You drove me in and never took a penny — thank you
(I never said it)

My blood worked in the pools and my hands worked in
The shop, selling overpriced toffee crisps to toffs on their
    Second hols
I drank so many Slush Puppies, I swear my brain froze the
    Summer over

The year previous, the High Street let me go
I lied about it and got the bus, lost money hiding
I wrote poems on the beachfront inside ice cream cones

In the summer of '09
We drove down to Grantham
(Or was it Newark?)

You bought me this Buzz Lightyear figure
That was painted silver
He never looked like that in the movies

We all got sick and watched some VHS'
That the owner left, degraded tapes
Of fairy-tales that never hit the silver-screen

Lovely Holibobs, you said
That still makes me sick
You can follow lines through

Destinations and broken stop signs
Question marks and hesitant colons
Decorate the room that I grew up in

Monosyllabic conversations:
Yes. Don't get me started.
I wish. We can't. Maybe.

In that September, I took nothing with me
You gave me a pizza cutter and some
White plates, a hug right on the threshold

But not one in the summer,
It was freezing
When we touched

I still remember the cloth
That you were wearing,
The same as any other

I used to write about burning
Flat irons and Sterling Dual capsule pops
The smoke of an old stove-top followed me

Your new hob is electric
I can't burn myself
Like I did

I cannot call my gas-rings *Home.*
Like the house and my iPhone
They are temporary

Like looking for a dance at three am in a club I hate
Whilst bodies roach around bodies each crying out
For some sort of route back home

We are waving each other's
Arms in a takeaway, smoking month-old rollups
Snowdust ash into polystyrene boxes

I want to write about burning again

WINDOWS

When we were young, I threatened to fall
out of our best friend's bathroom window
at half two in the morning
It must have been three-feet-by-three
You laughed, not derisive just

Sad

BROKEN BOTTLES

Still finding glass
On the floor
From that time
We broke a bottle

Laughed about it
All night and
Thanked God we
Drank all the wine

We didn't clean up
For over forty-eight hours —
Nowadays that could be
Two long shifts

YEARS AND YEARS

It's weird how it's the little things.
Like how that guy we liked on that show
however many years ago,
is playing a gig in town next week.

A lifetime back, I'd have asked you to come:
We could get drunk and sing along
We'd tag each other in those stories
We haven't sent anything for a while

When I see your face,
I double tap my glass
I think about your dog;
I hope he's still chasing butterflies

ON VISITING 'THE BOX'

We weren't allowed in 'the box'
Well, not *weren't allowed,* as such;
More, we had no reason to be at 'the box'
Same way we had no reason to be in the Tesco stockroom,
I suppose

So when my sister went to hospital,
And I was taken to 'the box', I didn't care
About my sister, just cared about my adventure
The knobs and buttons, twists and pulls

'The box' was a giant game of Bop It, and
If I pulled it, pressed it, yanked it right then
The passengers would be just fine: but if I pulled it,
Pressed it, yanked it, bopped it wrong,
A hundred men might die

'The box' is an anachronist: it felt wrong in the noughties
Today the wooden slides and slats
Are barely funded bric-a-brac
The last remnants of a cultural cul-de-sac

SCABS

for Rick Stevenson

He never would scab —
He's a good lad
Bite the hand that feeds
Coz you're the one he needs
Your labour is your power
Stand together, never sour

IN THE COUNTRY

In the country,
Restaurants ~~black out menus~~
With a bitter biro

Three odd clocks sit
On paisley walls
Twelve chintzy cats
Perch near chalk specials
Eyeballing the tea-drinker

There's a choice of Carling or wine,
Would Sir like red or white?

No-one is running from the rat-race
They have settled down on the track
And put their feet up in a two-up/
Two-down terraced place

And the eulogies
In the paper
Remind me of my
Sermons, and the old boy's
Conversations in the
Café remind me that since
We're all gonna die
We should try
Dying happy
Side-by-side
With people who'd
Happily split
Cheap cake and
Bad coffee

D£CL ı N3D

Declined again
You're kidding me —
Declined? Mate listen just
Get us this round
Yeah?
And the next
And I'll sort it
Pay you back
Tuesday
Got no food in,
Starving, Let's
Wander round
The girls' tonight, they'll
Knock us up some
Grub — yeah, you can
Come too, if you like

FREE WRITING

I will use the embers of these vowels as fuel to boil a kettle full of
North West water and pour scorn into my coffee browns / how
can anyone be Bukowski or Cummings, if entire cities are typing
notes every hour praying for forgiveness / How can anyone be
Hughes when there are so many giants upon which we all stand;
piling up poets would touch the outer atmosphere: We could pull
down commercial space flights together
If culture is a ball of string the cat got loose in the sixties and all
the milk cartons in the world cannot bring him back, like
Thatcher's Britain he has been snatched / I have anxiety about
my anxieties and at the dial tone I freeze / I don't even know who
I owe money
to and I need a reset
button because my twenties have been a mistake but
the ruptured lungs keep pushing for
more air, more time, more life
twitching on a knife line I'm strafing
round   corners
scared of what I might
find
I am free writing
I am free, writing
I am free

GARGOYLES

My Mum and Dad are trapped
In their mid-forties,
My mate Dave perpetually exists
In The Year Above
We haven't shared a courtyard for a decade

I wonder when the term *mid-life crisis* was invented,
and who it applied to:
When did we die? What was mid-life? If it was the 19th century,
I'd already be living mine.
If it was the 17th century, I'd almost certainly be dead.

I fantasise about the coming crisis:
Picture myself slinging second-hand sofas in Benidorm
I wish I wasn't so fucking moral
So I could go to a stag do in Majorca,
Get a tattoo of Woody from Toy Story on my arse
Work in accounting and
Underpay Jessica from HR
Intentionally every month
By a few pence
Not enough to argue over,
Just enough to make
Some significant difference to her
Long term prospects

This planet has definitely missed
Its mid-life moment and now we're all
edging towards a solitary hospice stay
Even Pluto abandoned us, and I'm pretty sure
Mars isn't the hold-your-hand-for-your-last-breath type

I wonder how many flies it would take to eat off all my skin
Once we're all dead and dancing
And I celebrate my potential as a host
I would make a fine Mexican banquet,
I would wear a small, straw hat on my skull
I would pour a generous shot of a mediocre spirit
for anyone who wants one.
I will haunt this fucking party
the same way the 80s haunt this country

Overall though,
If I died tomorrow
I don't think anyone
would piss on my grave.

So that's something.

STANDING ON A HILL AS A COW

Stand on a hill
Lie down if you think
It might rain tomorrow
Put your belly to the grass,
Spread your legs like a man
On a bus, in a pandemic
Look up
If you can.
Your sky is burnt orange,
Shepherd's warning-sign,
Your babe has gone.
Stolen from your arms
And you will cry
And if you had streaming,
You'd listen to Taylor's Versions
And you'd send a group text
And plan a bottomless brunch
And run, far, far
Away

CRAZY TAXI (2006)

For six years,
Three PM meant Ian,
followed by a plate of Skegness Noodles —
Instant, with bacon and sweetcorn

For six years
He was paid by the council
To take us half a mile
Down to school and back

In six years,
I'll be thirty-two,
With no kids and
A full plate of vegan Pad Thai

FROM A PRAYER BOOK
for what might have been

According to his prayer book
My Grandad was a Guardsman,
A Christian,
And an Addict.

Fredrick joined up in January
Nineteen Thirty-Seven
Two years before he had to
One of 200,000
After a week he had his
First Communion

There, he received a prayer book:
Page three invited soldiers
Add their own appeals
Filthy coffee sprinkled
Onto fodder-paper

Grandad survived the war
I know nowt more
He wouldn't talk about it
All he'd kept was his prayers

When we turned out his house
Bottles of booze
Betting receipts
In his bible
April's Luck
Summer's Sky
Ticks fly
Needlessly high
And a table
Of numbers
Each charting
His defiance

While he didn't
Always win
It moved
His mind
From the
Scribbles
He'd cross out
The page
Before

AIRBNB FOR A MONTH

You don't learn the Underground in a month,
But you might learn a routine
You don't get used to sharing someone's life
Golden rings, pancakes, filter coffee;
Everything adjacent to your catalogue
His spirit comes from a cafetiere, not a Nespresso machine

My host was an extra in everything:
He was in the Ministry of Magic,
He tells me one evening, over rosé
I'm in the background of Avengers:
Thor saved me with his hammer
He pours out black coffee
Whilst I Google tube maps
I can't remember where I lived now
I can only remember the daft tube stops:
Elephant and Castle (no elephant, no castle)
Aldgate (no gate at all, actually, definitely not an old one)
Burnt Oak (worrying)
Home never felt further North

THEY STOLE OUR SHOPS

He sits on a wall, red brick with missing filler. He taps out a slight message on a Sony Ericsson, asking what time to arrive. The shop around the corner is bright yellow, but it used to be bright red. He's not fully sure why, but even though it long since became 'Premiere' he'd kept calling it 'Jason's'; he knew his parents did too. He assumed the person inside probably was called Jason: that made sense.

He wonders why they were even interested in this sleepy half-town. Besides Jason's, there were three pubs, the skate park (two slopes and a wooden block), a pharmacist and another supermarket called 'Kwik E Mart'. 20th Century Fox never came calling; he doubted they ever would.

That Sony became a Samsung, became a second-hand iPhone; still the town slept. He sloped off the red brick and flicked a lighter into a large, raw flame. No one cared about this hole: you can still hear the void come calling from the abandoned train tracks.

THE SUN

When the sun
peeks   round our
regulation windows
the scars on your pockmarks
paint pictures that I'm scared of
I want to take your fears
Type them down
Print them out
Crush them up
Throw them out
But the printer's out of ink
You're thrown out of planes,
Fall straight into blazers,
I try my best for you

We're all looking for escape routes

HOT FUZZ

The first time I watched a
star crossed lovers' kiss
was in *Hot Fuzz*. I think
about that phrase,
I picture two families welded
together like ice-picks into
mountain-face,
fountain pens on offcut paper scraps
heartache in a cul-de-sac
a decade of fusion
cross country panic attacks
Romeo was only
fourteen after all
Just like you
A year before the baby-scare

ISN'T IT FUNNY THAT THEY KNEW IT FIRST

They used to wrap up otherness in a queer plastic bag, stick it on the top shelf, scribble *faggot* on it and keep it separate.

Keep the good stuff sterile.

I saw a comedian explaining that in America, it's the high school goths that started having sex first, because they just screwed each other, whilst the jocks (I suppose we would call them lads) were all too scared of Jesus, and their mothers. The difference, he said, was that the goths never got any social credit for it because they had blue hair. So — by and large — we kept separate. A secret society tucked inside a queer plastic bag on the top shelf.

When you shouted *fag* in the dinner hall queue for pizza, aged 14, I felt like a train with no conductor. *Does this service stop there? We've never been before. Sure, we've seen it on the sign, but we've never actually been there.*

So I, with my black nails and my straightened hair, shrugged. I figured that Gerard Way must know how this felt, so it was fine. Being bullied for being alternative is simply *de rigueur*, I thought. Standard practice. Everything in secondary school is. Life must move to the correct, precise ticks and tocks. It made sense in the same way my skinny jeans and upside-down cross made sense.

Five years is a long time to spend with the same people. By the end of it, I stopped painting my nails and I cut my hair into a quiff. I threw away my crucifix. I still wore skinny jeans, but nobody called me gayboy any more because everyone wore skinny jeans now and I got pissed in fields with people who used to stuff me on the top shelf. I sterilised myself.

Five years later, I realised the top shelf was where the good stuff lives and celebrated by bursting out of the cellophane in Canal Street.

BANG, SLOWLY

Ambiguity got shot in the head
Romance took a gun and put itself to bed
When everyone is on, all the time
No one stops and nowt's worth a dime
and no-one dies, and everyone lies
You gotta ask: *what kind of life is this*

CODE SWITCHING

My coffee order changes
Like my tongue and my posture

Black, no milk
Masc and tall
For business suits,
Betting shops and
Meeting people's parents

Iced, oat milk caramel latte
Bent over, arms askew
Sugared sweet
In pink dungarees and
Yellow eyeshadow, too

Flat white, no sweetener
When the rain dances
On my eyelids in a 5am
Malaise — hazy like the heavy
Autumn air

Espresso Martini
My weekend comes calling
In an ornate glass dress
Let your limbs hang out,
Let that tongue turn golden

EVERY TWENTY YEARS

Elvis is an anagram for Levi's and we all know
That anagrams are symbolic of what could have been
They've thinned out every last memory
to be pored over in boardrooms,
Sold back twice as loud
E-numbers, additives, and needle drops
There's only really 100 years on a loop
Or, there was —
I think we'll just live in 1979 forever now:
Flares and austerity and the death of
John Wayne, on repeat

THE SQUARE

This square is rarely empty
today it is a quiet carnival
a mum tells her kids kept close
babies, I love you so much

We were all the clergy
hand wrapped in hand
in the shadow of Saint Anne's
proudly-perched mockingbirds,

We are stunned by one another
lairy lads show us their skeletons
raising coffee cups to the sky
like pints at night

INVISIBLE INK

I choose not to read   because I don't like paper-towel endings,
Dragonfly sunsets,   wax afternoons,
doomed romances,   I chose not to see

REWATCHING ROPE

last summer i watched twelve hitchcock pictures
when ben hecht wrote the script for *rope*
did he write granger and dall as lovers?
Why does our breath catch at the back
when they barely hide the body?
why do I leave with so many new
questions?

ITALY, 2018
for Michaela, then and now

Vivid the speech
Spoken by all people
Potted plants in black sea
Eat Swarovskis with bad tea
Scholars and maggots
Both with dirty habits
Equal in their insurgency
Riot amid democracy
Miles ahead still slow
Coal heats the show

TAURUS CIDER, 2017
for Robin

I wanna spend the summer
Drinking Aldi lager with you
Getting pissed in public
Writing songs about how
We're all gonna die
But that doesn't
Mean we have to accept it

It doesn't matter what
You're drinking
If the tunes are right
And we've got a playlist
Packed with Aphex,
Kendrick and Dilla
And another for later
With Beach House and
Julien Baker

How are we supposed to
Concentrate on our futures
When there is so much
To laugh about right now

JEWELLERY BOX

I wanna take out your eyes
　　and carry them in a box
So I can see your blue skies
　　and keep 'em behind a lock
I wanna take out your heart
　　and keep it close to mine
So I can hear the rhythm
　　and keep tapping in time
I wanna take out your mind,
　　and keep it in a tank
So I can toddle down whenever
　　And admire it at the bank

ANOTHER NEW JOB, IN THREE HAIKUS

I. beginning

big smiles pressed shirts, hot
lattes in cute cups, bubbling
froth behind a desk

II. middles, quickly

six months later, ice
coffee from the pricey shop
alone in the queue

III. ending

Three lasting contacts
drink tap beers in a back room
rinse the glass, repeat

PLATFORM FIVE

dawn's drains are already clogged with loose
change and travel cards
our platform — slick with northern chaos —
bursts ambition and heartbreak from morning
dams into thin plastic coverings, sleet-thin snippets
of conversations alight and cascade into
b&m z-list covers forming CRT memories
that smell like diesel and steak bakes and
instant coffee and sweat all coalesced

if he's   running
for the 7:10 train
he's gonna miss it

i've been waiting for the 6:58 so i know how he feels
funny how that goes isn't it, like you're always running
for something that weren't never going to happen
the voice of god, siri's northern ai, tells me
that I've got another 8 minutes to go so I start to bet against
    urban accretion
to stay regulated
there's a crushed-up coke can
that's been sat here for
weeks and
it's grown to represent a lot for me so I hope *they* never take it
    away but then again
they always clean yesterday's metro old rags and soak up last
    night's blood from the lift doors

drunk twentysomethings somersault
from the manchester line swapping
stations with the besuited ghosts
that they will grow to be

and the sleet keeps dropping down and pouring and
we'll all be drowned soon so let's break the rules:
light a fag
drink the booze
stay the distance
get the wrong
connection
before
    we're
        gone

II.
LEAVING THE
STATION

When I left the station, things started looking up

LEAVING THE STATION

Cheeks receded
He bit, cap down
over sallow skins,
Rolled tight like the
cigarettes we never smoked
We didn't talk about class much,
stuck in the back coach
writhing against our self-conscious
common tongues:
British holidays
Milk and bread,
Small house, kept well-fed
Two kids, premium
Netflix subscriptions.
I get off at Salford Crescent,
Leave my lighter in the station

WOOLIES

I dunno, man
he sighs
from the back of his lungs
the kind of sigh that crawls
up throats and poisons tongues
I dunno, man:
Woolworths looks much worse in pictures

BOLTON TOWN, IN TWO PARTS

Part 1

It takes a village to raise a child,
A committee to raze a town to the ground

BHS, abandoned for four years,
still stares longingly at the
nineteen-nineties as he stumbles from the
betting shop into the thoroughfare

Industrial parks and chain shopping broke
the back of the browbeaten

I am the gentrifier
I raged against —
No oat milk here,
No egg replacement

The buildings are unlovable, rooted
Like the trees we burn down to kindle,
into magazines

What good will
poetry do when people are dying,
How many refugees will a museum hold,
the burnt out entrepreneurs of
the burnout generation
working eight/eight online,
harvest their spines for a filter coffee

I wonder what Steve
from Bolton, thinks when he looks at me,

moved here because it was cheap,
far cheaper than the city
not to own
(obviously)
to rent
Plus we wanted space
for a dog, and to build
a translucent life
until our parents die:
I suppose that buys us time.

Part 2

My local shopkeep is one minute away, at pace.
He's called Bhatt, though I'm not sure of his first name
I think he adopted a British one.
He co-runs the shop with two less-friendly men
He talks to me about India whenever I pop in for beer,
or off-brand ketchup, or vape liquid
I want to support the local economy but
as far as I can tell, there is one fully-vegan
takeaway in the whole town,
which is the largest in the UK
per-inhabitants

260,000 people live here, spread from
Farnworth to Halliwell, to Bromley Cross and Eagley.
There's posh bits, dire bits and everything-in-between bits.
There are three cinemas each a half-hour walk away
Each a chain, each showing the same films on a loop

We are well and truly in the trenches.

And every cafe still has an ashtray
You've seen that meme, with the sign,
Advertising good times like the 90's
Put your phone away and chat!
this is like that

Everyone says *hello*, asks if you're alright,
But the voice in the back of your head wonders
whether they are judging you, whether they think
you're actually not alright.

Your accent isn't Northern enough, your bleached-blonde hair
betrays ideas above your station. You wonder how much of a
prick you look with your AirPods in on the way to the station.

Everyone meanders through a town centre that, whilst it isn't
functionally awful, has no spirit.

It was Parliamentarian, surrounded by Royalists, and hosted a
massacre of the working class.

In 2021, a punk with pink, spiked tips, and the word *oosh* shaved
into his head fist-bumps an Austrian man named Marcus and a
Middle-Eastern bloke with a beard to die for.

This is not a gastro pub
The only thing that will kill it is us
A thousand year heritage turned into 'luxury' flats
I walk back to my house.
It is half the price of a two-bedroom flat in the city.

HALLIWELL

Blackened Quorn ham,
in day-before crusts:
a cheap-rent estate,
illegally-painted rust
chips with green mush
Argos and Starbucks,
twelve legs scuttle,
baked beans bust,
Always dead loud,
This house won't hush
Got big plans but
Not seen much
Dead big pans,
Cheap cookbooks,
Big old plants,
That still look lush

all of this is paper planes

The debt, the looks,
The bets, the books,
That set that makes
your bum look good,
The head, the hooks,
Your rail card, your Uber fraud,
Your stupid ex, your fears
and falls,
That slightly jammed door,
That queer eye twirl,
The weekend girl
Failed dates,
Wasted takeaways,
All paper planes
Diving onto
Paper plates

THE ESCAPE ROUTE

You ask me for a pen
every darkened morning
for a month straight:
take this, it's yours
keep it safe and jump —
England gives you sixteen years'
worth of plastic parachutes then tells you to
hand-glide over mountains without training
shimmy across the town we all grew up in
when the inspector calls at Christmas
we all eat from the same plate and pray
I ask you listen closely: you know you're good at this
I ask you your opinion: you say you've none to give
in a few months the state will cut the strings
I worry for your bright eyes
how we will all dull them
with fluorescent marketing
I know it makes no difference; your limbs can't
quite remember, your eyes don't quite connect
but you notice blues and pinks
you know that this is not fair
the sun is crawling up earlier
you keep giving me a reason
I'll keep giving you a pen

A NEW EYE APPOINTMENT, TOMORROW

the water has gone cold
but I don't want to get out
my knees are little mountains
with blue-black red caps
they wear them proud
like graduation gowns
they carry my weight
so i can carry yours
my eyes little bowling balls
reach in with your nails
scratch out dead weight
and throw them away
i will need a fresh pair
so tomorrow i can see

FACEBOOK SOFA

The window from the plane looks like a portal
I want to smash my fist through,
lick the bloody glass,
Remind myself we are more than bags of skin
The leather-red of second-hand sofas rests,
sagged with generations of exhausted sighs

In my living room, paws scratched into the crevices, like Robert
 DeNiro's bagged eyes.
It has seen traumas and tears, and joy, and children and it will
 see more again, just not here.

I can picture a future, for the first time, where I can purchase a
 couch, a sofa, and leave BHS, head held high.

It closed down years ago.

THE PRESSER

You're sat on the presser
The presser.
That's what I call it now
My language was dull and placid
till our tongues collided and now this
Love language is *the dog house*
And zombie films and *hot fuzz*;
My clipped and unsure accent has had
Babies with her Northern tea
I am gravy and flatlands
Rock City and romance;
She is seasides and mountain climbs,
Coconut milk and bright-pink hair dye
Acapellas in the bath, a B&M haul and
Another tote bag, back rubs, blue-grey whirlpools
Look alive. We've only got each other and our sofa.

FAKE FRIED CHICKEN

Just try it
I'm in a fake-dingy kitchen
in the centre of a city

Forty years ago,
it could have been
council blocks, this place

My mate takes his first bite
into the golden, molten crumbs
ears pricked, feline

Crack underneath his teeth,
pacer trains, threatening adventure
as the doors jam again

His pupils pop
excluded from the
whites of his eyes

He hops aboard for
the first time in his
life

It tastes so sweet
like levelling up,
like a lie

Which it is.

He sips a little lager,
scoffs a few chips and
leans in

Yeah, this is sick mate
he says over the din
these lies taste delicious
the promise that hard work
gets you a seat at the table

When places are already set
with four forks, two knives,
not for us to dine

They've speared a false
flag to the front of the line,
we'll queue politely with a smile

Watch as we scrabble
with our Wilko's cutlery,
to slice a little meat

From the bones
of a long-dead story
feed our families

Slow-roasted day old solidarity,
the wounds have scabbed
over each other's backs

We'll feast on benefit frauds
empty wards, recycling plans,
Muslim immigration, celebrity cancellation

In this place,
Every table is reserved
And your needs aren't met

They don't serve, except out back,
where they'll serve our heads

Find your nameplate
in the metal bin, mate

Thrown-out meal deals,
rotting land trash
tear tender flesh

From yourself
your set
your kin

They'll keep the
devilled eggs and
mango salads

We'll run riot
with a fork full'a

Batter

USING A CAFETIÈRE AS THERAPY
for the poets

When I lean down on the french press I
consider that therapy
And now it's been six hours since
and that therapy is sepia
When I am free-pouring black
coffee from the big, torn bag
left in the staff room
You teach yourself new habits quickly —
I have spun the two pence and ended up with heads
I have told tall tales and I press it again
against my chest
I nod at the cleaning staff and I am ashamed
by the state of my work room:
I have no energy to tidy it

Eleven hours since the cafetière

I'm in The Soup Kitchen and I
think about the millionaire backers behind it
The almost derelict walls and neon signs and the bare,
unmarked taps teasing beers and the bopping smiley heads
of other people swimming on a rising sea that tastes
like copper irony and how I'm one paycheque getting lost
away from drowning in a sea of zesty orange IPA

Fourteen hours since the cafetière

Wet Leg is on the speaker. We're all wet, too,
because it is dripping from the roof top
outside plumes of vape smoke us and Martin,
striped T-shirt, Adidas, said something about
me moving closer he's misheard me but
I don't correct him, I'm already in
The middle of another anecdote and we're all
Just trying to be funny and profound
And I wonder if everyone here will outlive me,
and I wonder if I everyone here hates me,
and I wonder if I'm talking too much about work,
and not enough about my perpetually impending career,
or not enough about work,
and too much about everything else
— and I can feel the brittle of my teeth decay when we lay back
tequila shots —
and I am not quite present
but all my friends are here

YOU CAN'T KILL A GHOST

I'm not going to kill myself
Spit these words at me
Season them with
Ground-up disgust,
Sprinkled rock-salt glances
Half-smiles flirting
In the fluorescence
I see your teeth:
I don't believe them.

You're upset at you
Who created four.
You're upset at me,
Who added two and two.

You are a battlefield
A war with two generals:
Today, the spectre made an advance
Her pale form drained of your extravagance
Tomorrow, the flesh and blood
will fight back.
Dancing in the drama of daylight;
The day after that,
You may think the war is over.

You cannot kill a ghost.

You may exorcise your ills
For weeks and months
But they remain your ills
You are your ghosts

You cannot run from them
For they will haunt you
You can only offer
Treaties to demons:

Split the bills,
Fill out forms,
Move them in.

Alongside your signature ski
To be traced by gentle hands
A reminder to look to the sky
Wave a flag, play your favourite
Songs and sing a long
Your voice is proof of
Wondrous, astonishing
Breath.

FIVE HOURS PER WEEK

i only see
five hours a week
that leaves one-hundred-and-
sixty-three
where i don't see
anything that happens
and the days for me
just keep on coming

so i take up my red pen and try
to unpick your brain,
why you are the
way you are
and why you can't
just be polite

at dinner time,
I saw you break a plate
and laugh
and at 2pm, you screamed
and threw a fit
and at 3pm
you took my pen

when i wrote my name
inside your planner
what wrote me back?
a tribute to a mother
and your older brother's scrawl
signed inside the bottom right
i remember his hand

he only left school last summer

STOP!

Stop scratching your beautiful face!
Stop screaming at the neighbours' place!
Stop looking so scary when I know you are soft!
Stop growling at all the other dogs!
Stop pretending to be something you're not!
Stop taking up the whole bed!
Stop reminding me that one day you will be dead!
Stop liking Friends! Stop hating Peep Show!
Stop walking so fast and stop running too slow!
Stop only eating the meat and refusing the brown balls!
Stop chasing next door's cat up the walls!
Stop greying so fast, you daft, fawn-fog gymnast
Stop, stop, stop.

FOR CHALKY
(found in a postcard)

We arrived today.
We miss you
already.

We've been swimming
so, so much.
We haven't left
the sea.

It's near the place
where we are camping
the pebbles twist
onto my skin
it doesn't hurt

Sent down through
breezes and bird-song
gently whispering,
a notice-board of
the extraordinary
world we inhabit

The mirror
image of you
is written in
the grains of sand
where I spread myself
not thinly, like the city's last tub of butter,
but lavishly

There is no worry
I shall run dry here

all these facets
of a planet I've
never considered
are reminders to
love myself

Like I love you

NEW GLASSES

At work
Everyone thinks I got some new glasses
I didn't
I picked all the plastic from the frame
I spent
Hours trying to piece my anxieties into
A shape
That people can view through unfiltered lenses
And say
Wow; that looks great. You pay a whack for something
Like that?
I picked all the plastic from the frame
Sorted out
The mire of the day over decaffeinated coffee

SENTENCES AND CLAUSES

The ink injected into you is not a sentence
But a clause
The little poems
That decorate your skin
Were chosen, deliberate
All the rest is just coincidence
Tattoos are an outfit for nakedness
Something to decorate your pale frame
I will still send a cake to
the curves of your hips
On your worst day
Whilst you may not fancy candles,
You can light up a room
In your mermaid skin

THE BEST SPAGHETTI IN THE WORLD

for Michaela

You make the best spaghetti bolognese this side of Venice
Though when we went, we never rated the food, really:
I suppose we didn't go to Bologna
This burst bag of Quorn mince might break an Italian's heart
You always use the freshest ingredients, except for that
Because you hate using anything on the turn
When you serve it, I wonder when our experiences divided
I live inside two thousand and five, nine years old, biting
Apples that were past ripe, thankful for small mercy
You have sent them to be condemned to a past life
Taking a dulled knife to anything from that time
Never touching anything I leave on the kitchen sides
You are a gourmet chef in a burger place, sighing
It's two thousand and eight and the Michelin places have gone
Bust, but McDonald's and Burger King are on the up
You take a job to pay the rent, and still
You make the best spaghetti bolognese this side of Venice

WHERE DID I LEAVE MY APATHY?

Apathy lives in the frosted windscreens of financed cars.

That slight hand that tugs at yours when you can't be arsed to put the bins out. The takeaway you can't afford, the cider you paid over market price for. Apathy stalks every home; it lives inside Spotify Wrapped and functional pop dancehall. The men in ill-fitting suits replaced your spinal cord with DVDs of Fast and Furious remakes. Remember, deep down, because you can find morals buried inside of CRT screens:

We want the finest wines available to humanity
We want them here
We want them now

ON TOP OF NOWHERE

A man's fingers should be calloused and rough. His mind should be fortified, like the box-wine his wife drinks. He should not dye his hair, he should not paint his nails, he should not dance in the moonlight nor ever really listen to the song. He should be a pint of Carling and he should shy away from the Asti. He should wear Gildan prints and drainpipe blues, live inside of betting shops and pub crawls and drug deals.

SILHOUETTES AND NEW PLANTS

I sketch a silhouette
On your inky arms
Breathe in your mint toothpaste
The air in our house is recycled
You bought more plants
I laughed at the delivery driver
When he dropped off the boxes
Brown paper and cardboard
With directions for safety
Keep upright
And smile

WAX NOTES

i have scoured the internet for top ten lists. I have listened to most of the compiled top-one-hundred albums to listen to before you die, but i keep returning to mediocre metal bands and kanye west. I like that one todd terje album, and i like jazz but i can never remember who played what on sketches of spain. i like reading about food but i keep returning to that one indian street-food place which is quickly becoming a chain. i don't want it to fail but the more it expands the more i feel like other people are living in a hotel that i had the run of; i used to feel like josé mourino staying at the lowry and now i feel like the barman at a travelodge serving drinks to beleaguered families who say goodbye at midnight, still in cheap suits and rare dresses after awkward weddings. i like social realism but sweet sixteen is still my favourite. i like ken loach but i can't remember the plots. i tell people i love foreign cinema but my favourite french film is la haine. at least it isn't amelie.

DEAR MR. BURNHAM

Dear Mr. Burnham,

It's been years now and I feel like we're going nowhere
I don't doubt your credentials, it's not that I don't like us but it's
more that I'm over this

It's not you, it's me; I've moved on
Party politics is in my rearview mirror, metaphorically speaking.
I am driving a throughline down the A666, wondering when the
   lines collided.

Yes, I'm breaking up with you and I realise that there are a
thousand worse men out there, but that doesn't mean we need to
share a wardrobe: I have barred the windows and doors and I
swear no men wearing blue rosettes will enter this home: you do
not need to worry about cheating.

I will probably vote for you again, but I
can't spend another day knocking on a door with you
when there's still broken faces on Piccadilly Approach
I can't agree with the high rises when Hulme is middle class

I can't pin my hopes on a single election when everything else is
   on fire
You're the smiling face behind the police presence in EAL
   majority high schools.
You can throw a dart at the city centre and walk for fifteen
   minutes to find some poverty: barista's who can't buy coffee,
   rail workers picketing and you're no where near the scene
Landlords with old money attend mixers and laugh at landlords
   with new money, the servant class weeps because the cheapest
   wine in the goblets atop glass trays costs a week's wages for a
   drop

It looks like their blood
it smells like their blood
it tastes like their blood

Mr. Burnham, have you ever tasted servant blood?
Mr. Burnham, I am sure that you could

I don't want your skyscrapers and I don't want the nineties
I don't want crime and I don't want vanilla lattes
in Salford shopping city

Where is your decency
What happened to the little people
Capital letter North West water
squirms out of battered scumflick taps
I wonder if you've seen these air bubbles for half a decade.

I want to cut Manchester out of the map and keep its corpse
in my kitchen. The hacienda plays on whilst I chop mushrooms
The remains of Salford watches Netflix in my living room:
Media City is a parlour act designer cat
perched on the windowsill
One great city state is a thousand-corpse failure,
Overlays on the peeling plastic face-fronts of my terraced house
where real people live, I wonder how exactly it came to this

Mr. Burnham
I feel like we're going nowhere

BIG SOCIETY

An impromptu
Communion of fag butts
Floating together
In a Maccie's cup

SURPRISING STICKERS

A Conservative Party sticker,
A Manchester lamp:
Vote blue to kill your friends

NEON KNIGHTS

Tuckers
24-hour
Criminal lawyers.
Neon-purple sign
No sign of entry
Scaffolding next door,
No-one goes in
No-one comes out
Always has been,
Always will be
You really don't want
A lawyer at 3am

I NEARLY NEEDED A LAWYER AT 3AM
for Maty Moody

In retrospect, I have been waiting for this. It's a god-damn miracle it never happened before, really, and you can sure bet it isn't ever falling out of my skull now. It was five past three in the morning: dawn breaking in a few short hours, but for now it's all-nighters, flicking lighters outside a kebab shop.

Let's be clear: I've been antagonising bouncers since 2013. Thin as a whippet who missed breakfast, with the muscle mass of a Lowry speck, there's still something addictive about throwing my guts after any old bone. The most delicious, though, are those bowled overarm by bigots.

They chuck 'em out, I chomp em down. Can't help it.

Injustice, that's what gets me going. Racist old ladies at train stations. Homophobic idiots flicking spittle into the abyss. Chucking out at boozers without cause. Stolen cider. Bus drivers being arsey about someone's declined card. Prima Donnas in Superdrug: wherever the jackboot of authority strikes, I'm on hand to make a snide comment about the poor-quality leather finish. The real-life embodiment of cancel culture: I won't actually do anything, but be damn sure: I will be on hand to dole out pithy comments. Classy.

So, naturally, a three am verbal scrap sounds like a plan, especially after pints. I'm with close mates when we vacate Blackdog Ballroom. The evening, so far, has been successful: overplayed nineties hits mixed with the right level of spiced rum, vaping on the dancefloors, running from security. I'm still in my work gear: a hoodie pulled over suit trousers. Inconspicuous. Now, my best mate Matt is proper tall. Over six two, with the weight of a former rugby player. He's patient. The kind of patient that never takes a huff with the call centre, because he knows they're just following protocol. The kind of patient that understands that delays on the rail system aren't just standard, they are inevitable and that the root cause of the issue isn't the miserable, balding conductor, but the miserable, balding transport secretary Grant Shapps.

The kind of patient you want to test.

Let's rewind back forty minutes: 2:25. I Bet You Look Good On The Dancefloor seemed like a calling card: iPhone falls to sticky trampoline floors; my eyes blinking, all neon lights and Jägermeister. iPhone dies, nowhere in sight. Fuck it, it's insured. Tequila blinds after all. Now, Matt's gone too. Fuck knows where, but this is a banger coming in, and he's probably just at the bar. Eyes down, keep dancing.

So we keep bopping. Time flies till, like the Dark Knight in flares, he arrives back: eyes rolled so back it's all white, no iris. Hands me a grey, metal rectangle.

"Behind the bar. Twat."

I hugged him, tight, the kind of hug you only give after being called a twat. I move a little bit like a six foot cheese string. Peeling out from Matt's body, I collide with his plastic cup: vodka coke spills onto our shoes, mixing with the small pools already soaking the dance floor. I laugh, he doesn't.

2:45. Bobbing and weaving from the bar to the exit, fifty quid down and too many tequila shots later, a cloud of vape smoke follows me like a halo. Head count: all present and mostly correct.

Wallet, keys and (miraculously) phone — all on deck. All smiles, we wander over to a Northern Quarter takeaway, the kind that hangs hazy in memories and abandoned plastic boxes that sit on kitchen sides for too long. The sheen of the Cultural Quarter is sandpapered off at night; Coke cans, piles of sick and abandoned baggies line our path. On Lever Street, I take a run up to a wheelchair access ramp to a closed kebab shop and launch onto Matt's shoulders, laughing like a man possessed.

"Stop it."

Patience unties my hands from around his neck and replaces them with a clear, verbal red line.

"Stop jumping on me. I'm pissed and fucking fed up with you."

Meanwhile, a bouncer in her late 30s shouts *grow up* at me from a distance. Instead, I throw up a middle finger, knowing even then that this was uncalled for.

We're getting closer to the enticing smell of the chippy. I am led by my nose, and buzz around, like a puppy on its first walk.

The rest of them wince when I bounce up to Matt again.

"What you gonna get!?"

Bobbing round each side of his face.

"What?"

Left.

"You!"

Right.

"Gonna!"

Left.

"Geeeeeet?!"

Innocuous, simple, annoying.

Jump. Up, on to broad shoulders.

Climb down, laugh off, walk away.

The night's noise slows. Then, in whirlpool, everything goes down. Rugby player jumps onto Lowry reject, all collide with the floor, elbows first.

Immediately, apologies hang in the air like cigarettes. Arms around necks like football players saved from relegation: there's no exuberance, it's all one level from regret. Life didn't quite flash before anyone's eyes, but sometimes you don't learn shit, 'til you're shoved down into it.

THANK YOU FOR TRAVELLING WITH US

I suppose my concern is that this well has broken now, and I can't return to it. I wonder: if we continue down this path, by the time I come to write again I will have said all I can about my relationship with class, money and with place. I worry that my relationship will continue to sustain, that I will continue to be happy, because there are only so many love poems you can bare to read. I suppose now I will have to own the term *poet*.

When I started doing this, I told my Dad it was *performance spoken word*, kind of like comedy. But now this book exists as tangible proof that I am a writer; I can not rely on the dull twinkle of performance; these words exist here until the world explodes and I will always own them. You will always own them, until eventually this arrives in an Age UK and I write a poem about serendipity.

I may not always agree with everything I have written and that is okay. Some of these poems are entirely accurate, others are life drawings, others are entirely opaque. I do not know who I will be tomorrow. I hope he is happier than the person that wrote the oldest poems here; I hope he is less self-centred than the person who wrote some of this nonsense. I hope he continues to make other people happy.

I wrote about my girlfriend, who inspires me every day. I wrote about my dog. I love her; she's mental. I wrote about my family; I hope they forgive me.

ACKNOWLEDGEMENTS

A special thank you to Rebecca Kenny at Bent Key for allowing this collection to happen. For a very long time, I thought of myself as a comedy poet, a stand up poet, a performance poet, a spoken word artist: anything but a page poet. I know now that I can be both.

Thank you to Michaela Violet, for inspiring me every day, and supporting wholeheartedly every single daft new project I come up with.

Thank you to my brother, Ben, and my friend Zoë for proof-reading various drafts of this thing.

Thank you to my family, Rick, Andrea and Ellie for providing me with enough stories to write about.

Thank you to anyone I cancelled plans on in order to work on this. I probably made up a better excuse at the time.

ABOUT THE AUTHOR

Will Stevenson is a queer artist working across spoken word, page poetry and hip hop. You can find his music streaming everywhere under the name Will Switchblade, and you can attend Switchblade Society, a night he co-runs with Michaela Violet, in the basement of The Peer Hat in Manchester every third Sunday of the month.

ABOUT BENT KEY

It started with a key.

Bent Key is named after the bent front-door key that Rebecca Kenny found in her pocket after arriving home from hospital following her car crash. It is a symbol — of change, new starts, risk, and taking a chance on the unknown.

Bent Key is a micropublisher with ethics. We do not charge for submissions, we do not charge to publish and we make space for writers who may struggle to access traditional publishing houses, specifically writers who are neuro-divergent or otherwise marginalised. We never ask anyone to write for free, and we like to champion authentic voices.

All of our beautiful covers are designed by our graphic designer Sam at SMASH Illustration, a graphic design company based in Southport, Merseyside.

Find us online:
bentkeypublishing.co.uk

Instagram & Facebook   @bentkeypublishing
Twitter   @bentkeypublish